SUPER BOWL CHAMPIONS
KANSAS CITY CHIEFS

DEFENSIVE BACK
ERIC BERRY

SUPER BOWL CHAMPIONS
KANSAS CITY CHIEFS

AARON FRISCH

CREATIVE EDUCATION

Published by Creative Education
P.O. Box 227, Mankato, Minnesota 56002
Creative Education is an imprint of The Creative Company
www.thecreativecompany.us

Design and production by Blue Design
Art direction by Rita Marshall
Printed in the United States of America

Photographs by Getty Images (Vernon Biever, Jay
Biggerstaff/TUSP, Stephen Dunn, James Flores, Focus on
Sport, Rod Hanna/NFL, Tom Hauck, Wesley Hitt, DAVE
KAUP/AFP, Jason Miller, Panoramic Images, Joe Robbins,
Tim Umphrey)

Library of Congress Cataloging-in-Publication Data
Frisch, Aaron.
Kansas City Chiefs / Aaron Frisch.
p. cm. — (Super bowl champions)
Includes index.
Summary: An elementary look at the Kansas City Chiefs
professional football team, including its formation in
Dallas in 1960, most memorable players, Super Bowl
championship, and stars of today.
ISBN 978-1-60818-378-4
1. Kansas City Chiefs (Football team)—History—Juvenile
literature. I. Title.

GV956.K35F75 2014
796.332'6409778411—dc23   2013010567

First Edition
9 8 7 6 5 4 3 2 1

DEFENSIVE END
TAMBA HALI

OTIS TAYLOR / 1965–75

Otis was a tall wide receiver. He scored a touchdown to help Kansas City win Super Bowl IV.

TABLE OF CONTENTS

JAN STENERUD / 1967–79

Jan was a kicker who was born in Norway. Some people think he was the best NFL kicker ever.

JAN STENERUD:
YAHN STEN-uh-rood

THE MIGHTY CHIEFS

In 1963, a football team called the Texans moved to Kansas City, Missouri. Many American Indians used to live in Missouri. So the Texans became the Chiefs!

HANK STRAM / 1960–74

Hank was a smart coach for the Texans and Chiefs. He led the team for its first 15 seasons.

WELCOME TO KANSAS CITY

Kansas City is in the middle of the United States. It is famous for its many water fountains. It is also famous for a special kind of barbecue!

11

DEFENSIVE END
NEIL SMITH

NOISY ARROWHEAD

The Chiefs' home is called Arrowhead Stadium. It is one of the noisiest stadiums in the National Football League (NFL). The noise can make it hard for opposing teams to play there.

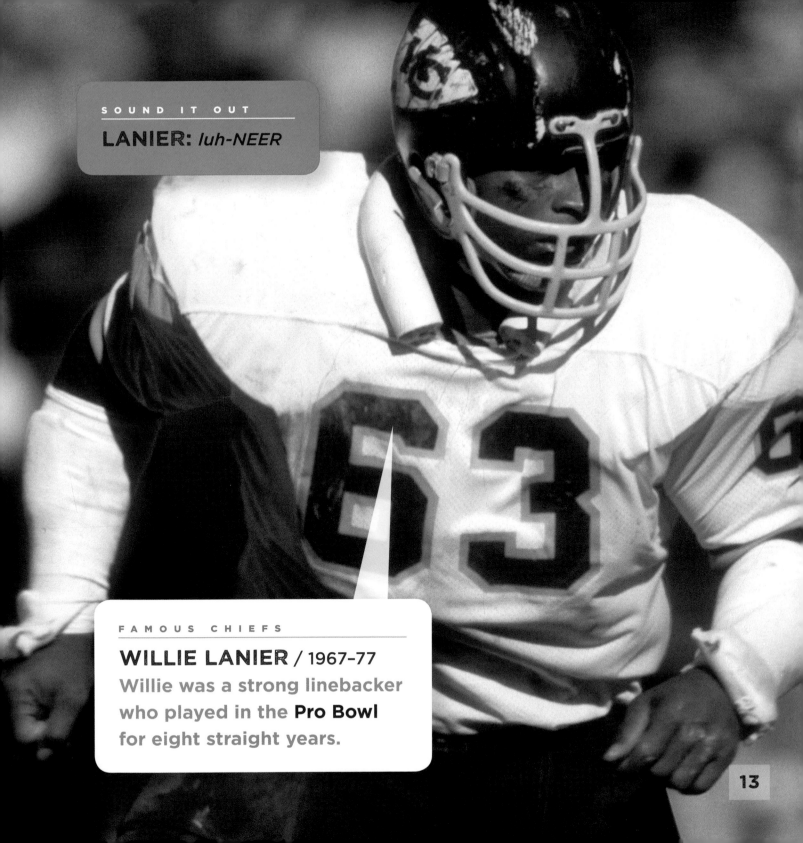

SOUND IT OUT
LANIER: *luh-NEER*

FAMOUS CHIEFS

WILLIE LANIER / 1967-77
Willie was a strong linebacker who played in the **Pro Bowl** for eight straight years.

"You have to have a great deal of help and I had the help all the way along the line."
— LEN DAWSON

THE CHIEFS' STORY

The Chiefs started out in 1960 as the Texans. They played in Dallas, Texas, as part of the American Football League (AFL). In 1962, the Texans won the AFL championship.

The Texans became the Kansas City Chiefs in 1963. Quarterback Len Dawson helped the Chiefs get to the very first Super Bowl. They lost that game, but they won Super Bowl IV (4)!

LINEBACKER/END
BOBBY BELL (#78)

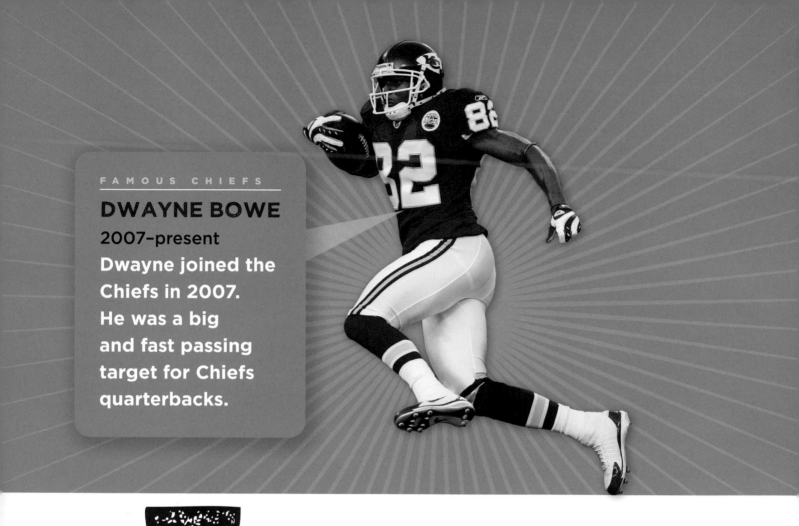

DWAYNE BOWE

2007–present

Dwayne joined the Chiefs in 2007. He was a big and fast passing target for Chiefs quarterbacks.

The Chiefs were not great in the 1970s after they joined the NFL. But they got better in the 1980s after stars like linebacker Derrick Thomas joined the team.

DERRICK THOMAS

17

"Life is short. You better get out there and do what you want to do while you can."

—TONY GONZALEZ

TAMBA HALI:
TAHM-buh hah-LEE

TAMBA HALI

Tight end Tony Gonzalez caught a lot of passes to help the Chiefs make the **playoffs** after the 2003 and 2006 seasons.

The Chiefs' defense got tough after Kansas City added players like defensive end Tamba Hali. Tamba was a powerful **pass rusher**.

By 2013, quarterback Matt Cassel was the leader of the Chiefs' offense. Kansas City fans hoped that Matt's passing would power the Chiefs back to another Super Bowl!

RUNNING BACK
JAMAAL CHARLES

FACTS FILE

CONFERENCE/DIVISION:
American Football
Conference, West Division

TEAM COLORS:
Red and yellow

HOME STADIUM:
Arrowhead Stadium

SUPER BOWL VICTORY:
IV, January 11, 1970
    23–7 over Minnesota
    Vikings

NFL WEBSITE FOR KIDS:
http://nflrush.com

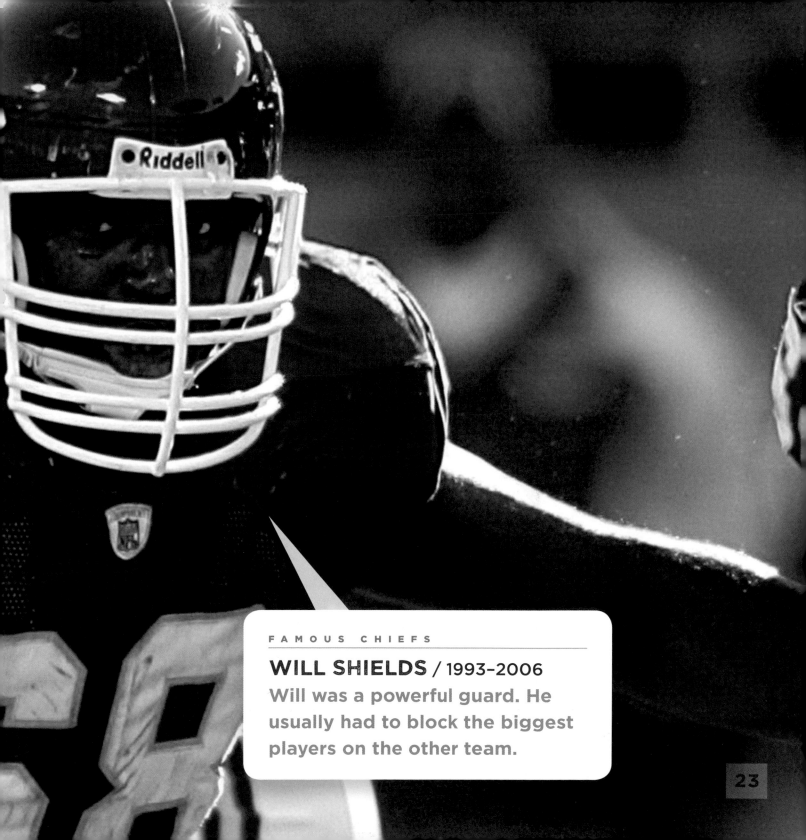

WILL SHIELDS / 1993–2006

Will was a powerful guard. He usually had to block the biggest players on the other team.

GLOSSARY

pass rusher — a defensive player who tries to tackle the quarterback before the quarterback can throw a pass

playoffs — games that the best teams play after a season to see who the champion will be

Pro Bowl — a special game after the season that only the best NFL players get to play

INDEX